Merry Ch—

Ken

Lots of love

Andy & Sue

Setting Sail

for the New Millennium

by
Ian Macdonald-Smith

To Douglas Anfossi, superlative seaman, constant inspiration,

tickled soul, great friend and sorely missed.

To the many lost at sea,

May their spirits sail peacefully.

Foreword

I cannot think of a harder challenge in the world of sports publishing, than to get the Tall Ships 2000 into one book. The range of ships and yachts in the fleet is so wide and there are so many of them. There are literally thousands of sailors from dozens of nations, and then there are the ports and cities where the race calls in, offering such a dramatic spectacle. No wonder the general public come flocking to every port, to admire the majestic square riggers, to watch the activity down by the quayside, and to soak up the romance and spirit of adventure which permeates the whole event.

Clearly it is impossible to cover every aspect of the race, or even to do full justice to every competing vessel. The mission of this photographic and descriptive book must be to create a record, which will be recognised by sailors and organisers alike, to capture the spirit and unique atmosphere of the race. To one and all, when they pick up the book and start flicking through the parts of the race they each remember best, they will say to themselves "I was there and these pictures bring it all back to life, as if it was only yesterday." If this book can succeed in such a subjective way for each person involved in Tall Ships 2000, then it will have succeeded in a big way for the event itself.

I should explain how I was offered the pleasant task of writing the foreword to the book. Ian Macdonald-Smith, the author and photographer from Bermuda, is my cousin, who was keen to have someone from the world of sailing to put a few words inside the front cover. We have both spoken to the ISTA a few times, not meaning to create confusion, but succeeding all the same. Although our names are the same, for which we can thank our parents, there is the subtle matter of the spelling of Ian and Iain, which we think makes us different, but in reality only causes even more confusion for everyone else. So from Iain to Ian, I am honoured to join this Tall Ships 2000 celebration.

I enjoyed watching the fleet leaving Southampton on 16 April 2000, in atrocious weather and an unusual south-easterly wind, which made it impossible for the square-riggers to sail through Spithead and between the Solent Forts. That must have been so frustrating for all the proud crew members and their families. The start of the race coincided with the tragic death of the ISTA Chairman, Robin Duchesne, who was also Secretary General of the Royal Yachting Association. His boundless energy and infectious enthusiasm for everything he got involved in, are greatly missed by all his friends and colleagues in the sailing world. He always had a twinkle in his eye, and he was the complete antithesis of the pompous administrator in sport, an example to the whole world of sailing of how our sport can be governed. He was a great sport and at the same time, a great asset for the sport.

The primary emphasis of the Tall Ships races is on youth, to foster the spirit of adventure and self-reliance among sailors between the ages of 15 and 25. These qualities come from sharing success and adversity, solving problems in a group, learning the qualities of leadership, learning the basics of seamanship, and feeling the pride of belonging to a team. There is no doubt that living in cramped quarters, sharing the duties of cooking and cleaning, working together to squeeze that extra tenth of a knot of boatspeed from trimming the sails to perfection, are all experiences which last a lifetime. The old-fashioned phrase "character building" sums up this whole experience, and it is hard if not impossible to find any other sport or occupation which develops these human attributes in a such a short space of time, with such lasting effect.

Rain or shine, in gales or glassy calm, the sheer fun and the physical challenge of sailing across open water in a racing environment, and learning to work as a team in an unfamiliar watch system, explores the depths of any human being. These are the tough days which stay in the sailors' minds and in their whole character. It is truly an indelible experience because it consumes every waking moment on the voyage. Afterwards, the best moments live on in our dreams, waiting till the next time.

I hope this book will help the next time to come round even sooner.

Iain Macdonald-Smith
Meonstoke, Hampshire
March 2001

Tall Ships 2000

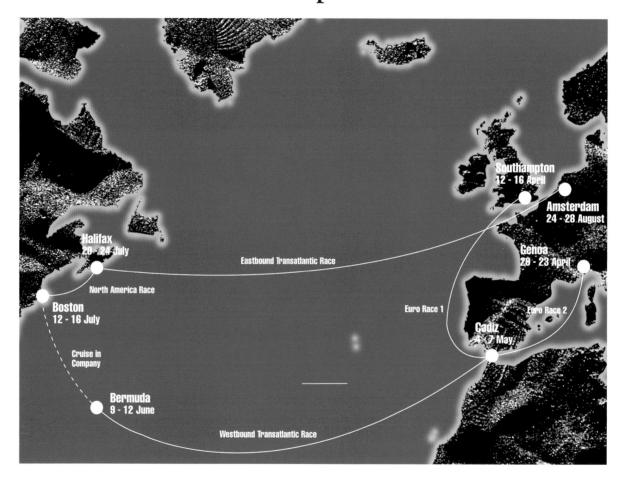

Southampton
12 - 16 April

Amsterdam
24 - 28 August

Genoa
20 - 23 April

Halifax
20 - 24 July

Eastbound Transatlantic Race

North America Race

Euro Race 1

Euro Race 2

Boston
12 - 16 July

Cadiz
4 - 7 May

Cruise in
Company

Bermuda
9 - 12 June

Westbound Transatlantic Race

Introduction

It was billed as 'the tall ships' race of the century' and 'the youth event of the millennium year'… and so it was. Seventy five sail training 'tall ships' from 25 countries took part in the 10,000 mile race. 7,000 young people, aged between 15 and 25, and from nearly 30 countries, made up most of the crews. Some 14 million people visited the seven ports when the fleet was in. And media coverage worldwide was colossal – print, radio and television coverage in over 30 countries, and the Tall Ships 2000 web-site peaked at over one million 'hits' a week.

The International Sail Training Association (ISTA) began planning for Tall Ships 2000 almost ten years before it happened. A course was selected to fit with the prevailing winds and currents. Seven ports were chosen to host the event along this course. A management team was put together. Help was enlisted from national sail training organisations, notably the American Sail Training Association. Sailing and racing rules were written. Budgets were prepared and funding secured. Sail training ships and boats of all sizes, ages and rigs were recruited. The event was also blessed with a glittering assembly of Patrons: Her Majesty Queen Elizabeth II of the United Kingdom, His Majesty King Juan Carlos of Spain, Her Majesty Queen Beatrix of the Netherlands, and His Excellency Carlo Azeglio Ciampi, President of the Italian Republic.

ISTA knew what had to be accomplished to make Tall Ships 2000 a success. After all, it had run races for sail training tall ships in European waters, from the Baltic to the Mediterranean, annually for over 40 years. But the prize for effort, commitment and the ability to meet the challenge of a lifetime certainly went to the owners and masters of the participating fleet and not least their young crews.

Sailing and maintaining any vessel on a 10,000 mile passage, preparing for and coping with the wild extremes of weather guaranteed in the north Atlantic, planning and provisioning, recruiting crews and organising crew changes at the various ports – all this placed incredible logistical and not least financial demands on those involved. But at the end of the race not one of them thought it had not been worth it, and all returned with fine memories, new friends, and great tales to tell for the rest of their lives.

Two fleets assembled for Tall Ships 2000 – one gathered in blistering sunshine in Genoa, Italy, the other under cold and stormy skies in Southampton, England. They all set sail in late April for Cadiz, Spain, and could hardly have had different experiences en route. Clear and windless skies frustrated those who started in the Mediterranean, while gale-force winds, hail and mountainous seas pummelled the northern fleet for most of its passage.

Cadiz was a welcome respite as the fleet prepared for the first Atlantic leg of the race to Bermuda. Again, mixed weather and even more mixed fortunes bedevilled the fleet; but every vessel made it to harbour, celebrating success or licking wounds. Bermuda was the crowning conclusion of the first half of Tall Ships 2000.

From here, a cruise to Boston on the north east coast of America with much of the fleet stopping at several ports along the eastern seaboard from Charleston, South Carolina, north, including for most of the fleet New York and its spectacular 4th July Independence Day celebrations. Then a race to Halifax, Canada, starting in a Boston fog so dense that on the big ships you could barely see from one end to the other, but ending in the sunshine and generous warmth of a Nova Scotian welcome. Finally, the long haul back across the Atlantic through more terrifying storms and debilitating calms to Amsterdam, the Netherlands – mid-August, four and a half months after the start.

Congratulations to all those who braved this great adventure. Hats off to the host ports as well. All seven turned on a great carnival atmosphere for the fleet, their crews and the millions of visiting tourists. Most of them also remembered that the whole purpose of the event was to promote sail training for young people and, through this, international understanding and friendship. Bermuda and Halifax in particular used the event to promote and develop sail training in a big way – each funded the participation of close to 200 young trainees in Tall Ships 2000, pledged to provide trainees for future races, and raised funds towards the building of their own sail training ships.

Tall Ships 2000 provided a valuable, perhaps even life-changing, experience for the thousands of young people who took part in it, and the fleet certainly drew crowds of awe-struck admirers in every port of call. Ian Macdonald-Smith captures the magic of Tall Ships 2000 through his lens in a way that few others have, and presents it in this fine book in a way that no-one else has. It will contribute to keeping alive the memories of those who were involved in the event, and it will surely inspire those who were not.

Nigel Rowe ~ Chairman
International Sail Training Association
March 2001

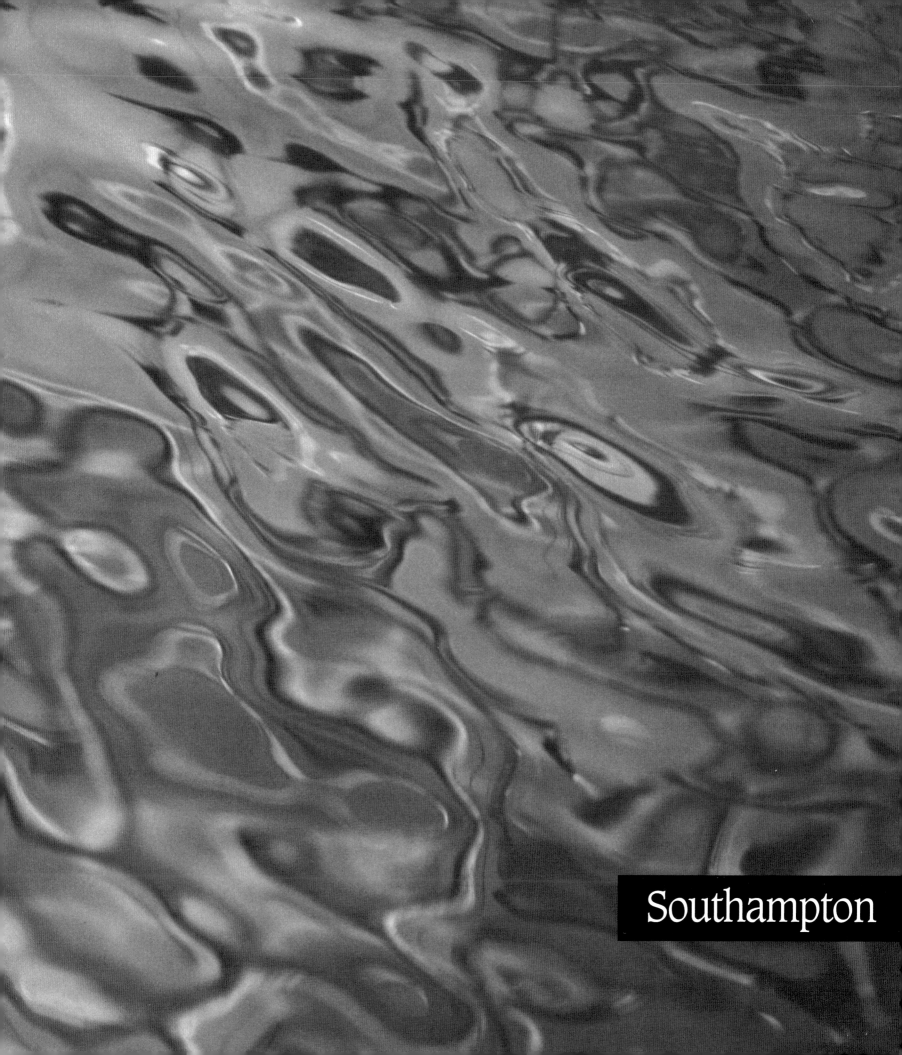

Southampton

Southampton from the Foremast of *Mir.*

From the rear *Iskra, La Recouvrance, Swan fan Makkum, Stavros Niarchos.*

Crowds enjoying the festive atmosphere on the waterfront with *Sedov* in the foreground.

Viewing Southampton on the day of departure from the rigging of *Mir* with *Kruzenshtern* in the foreground.

Repairing sails on *Eye of the Wind*.

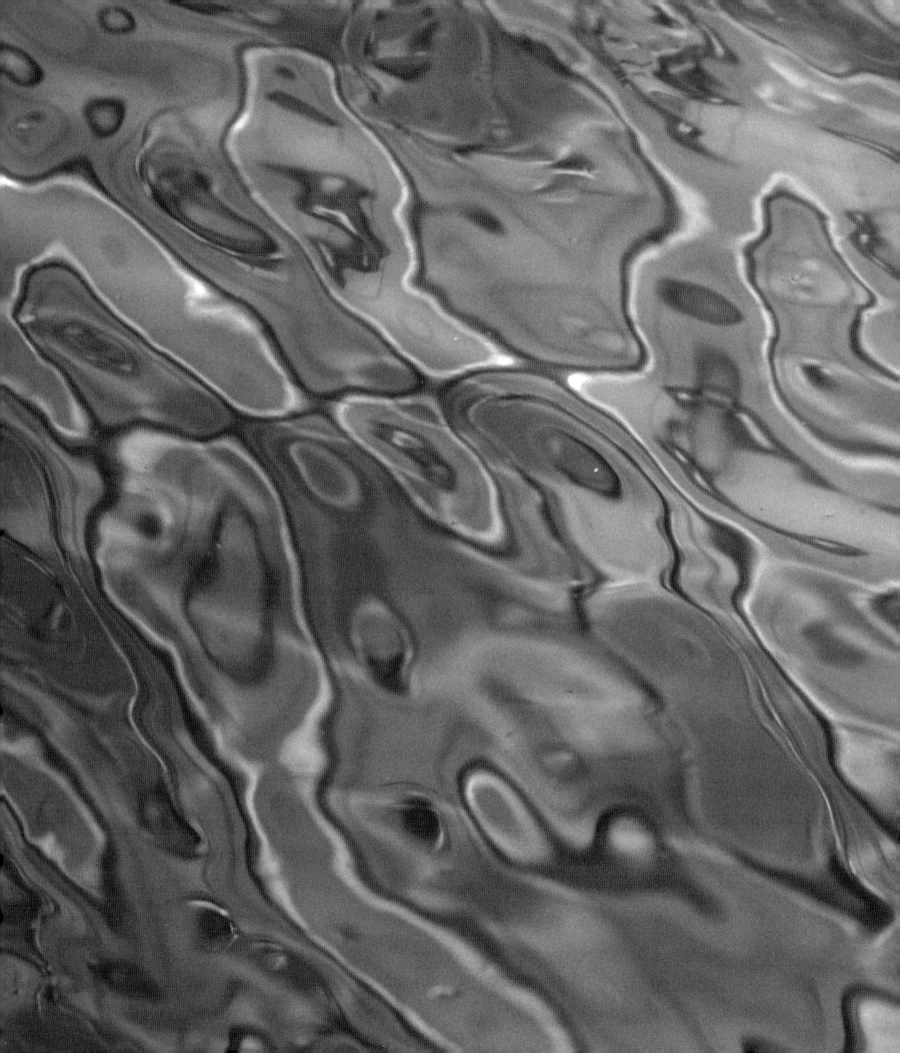

Underway in Southampton Water.

Hauling lines in unsettled conditions aboard *Lord Nelson*.

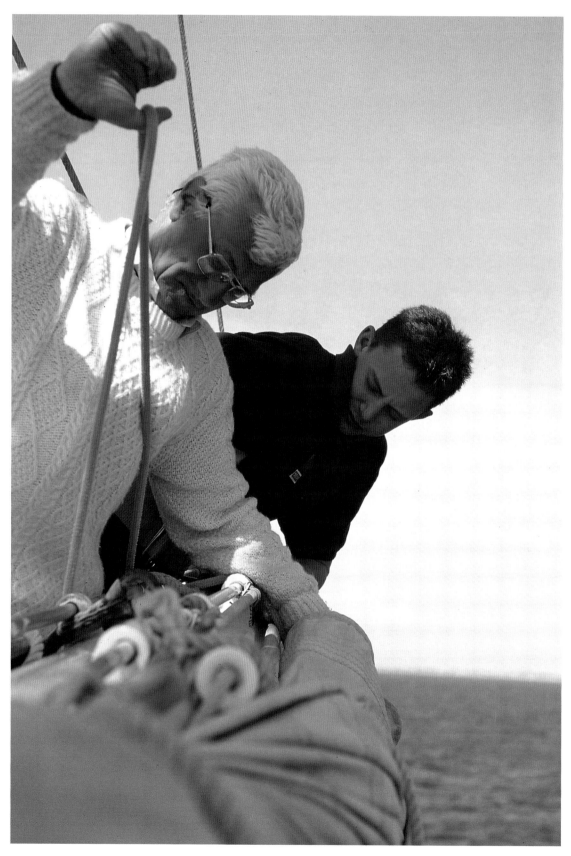

Demonstrating how to furl and gasket a sail at sea.

Handicapped and able-bodied sailors working side by side.

An uncommon waterspout off the coast of Spain.

Nearing Cadiz under full sail.

Genoa

Hanging out in the relaxed atmosphere of Genoa.

Polishing the brass aboard *Palinuro*.

Cadets sail training in the rigging of *Palinuro*.

Preparing sails aboard *ONO Ciudad de Cadiz*.

Organizing provisions for the journey to Cadiz.

Playing to the evening crowd.

An illuminated *Palinuro* resting calmly in harbour.

Serenading *Arung Samudera* on departure from Genoa.

Amerigo Vespucci leaving familar waters.

Kaliakra setting sail for Cadiz.

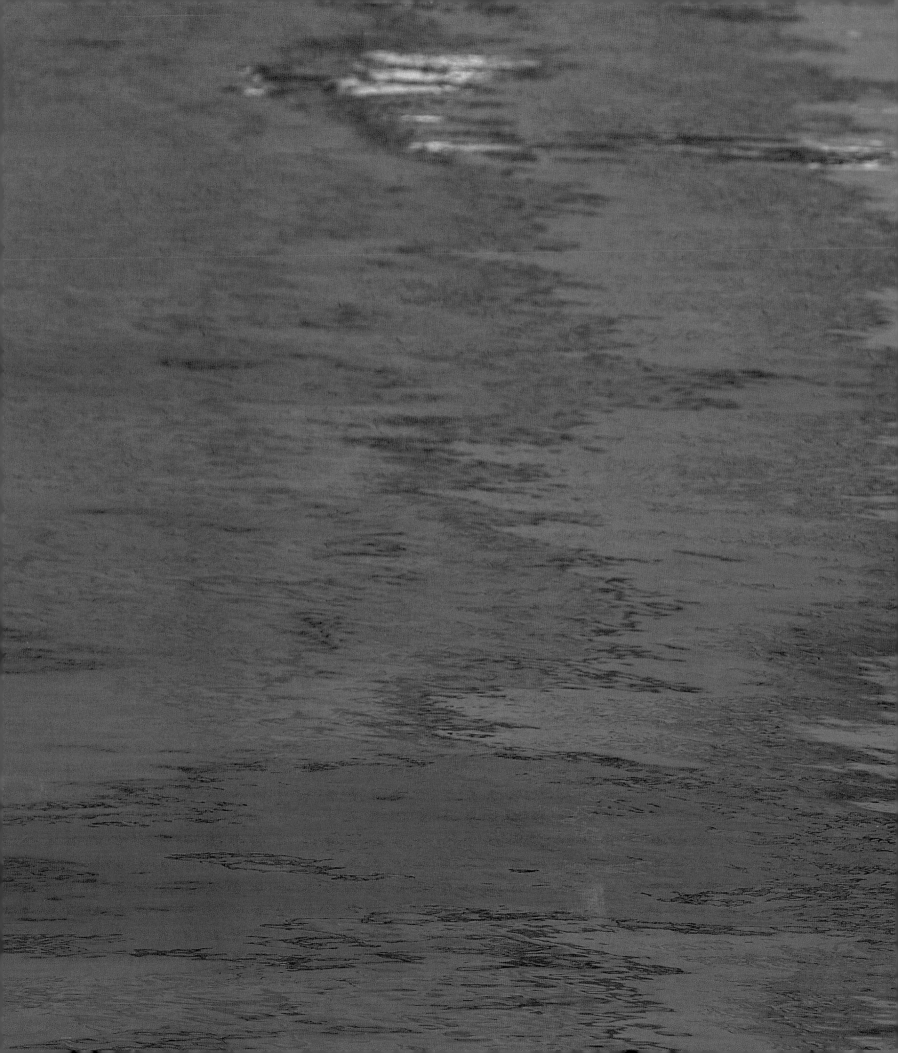

Cadiz

Amerigo Vespucci docking alongside *Juan Sebastian de Elcano.*

Loading *Juan Sebastian de Elcano* with fresh produce.

Preparing the gangways of *Amerigo Vespucci*.

Rinsing the hull.

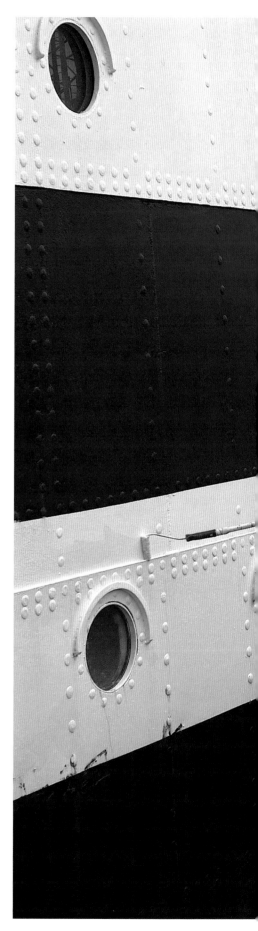

And painting it shortly after.

Laura Craik varnishing *Eye of the Wind's* aft deck rail.

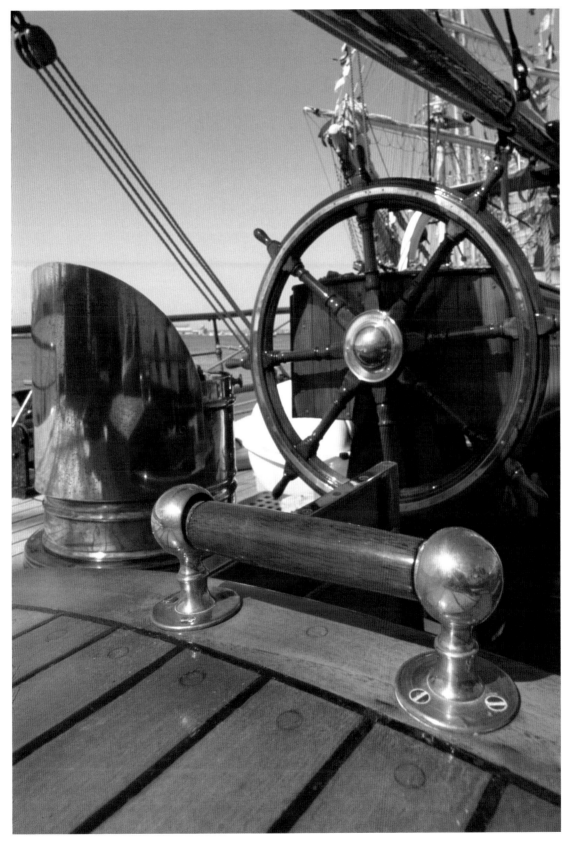

The exquisite aft deck of *Eye of the Wind*.

Detail aboard *Roald Amundsen*.

Mir's helm.

Details of *Kruzenshtern.*

Ship's bell on the foredeck.

Fife rail and main mast.

Watch muster.

Helm station.

Anticipating shore leave.

Turk's Head knots on *Europa*'s wheelbox reflecting colours of the Netherlands flag.

Painting *Mir's* hull.

The fleet basking in port, ready and provisioned for the Atlantic crossing.

Seeming chaos of masts and rigging.

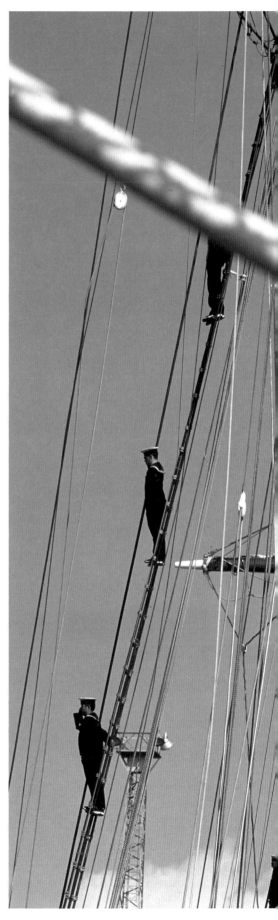

Manning the Yards of *Juan Sebastian de Elcano*.

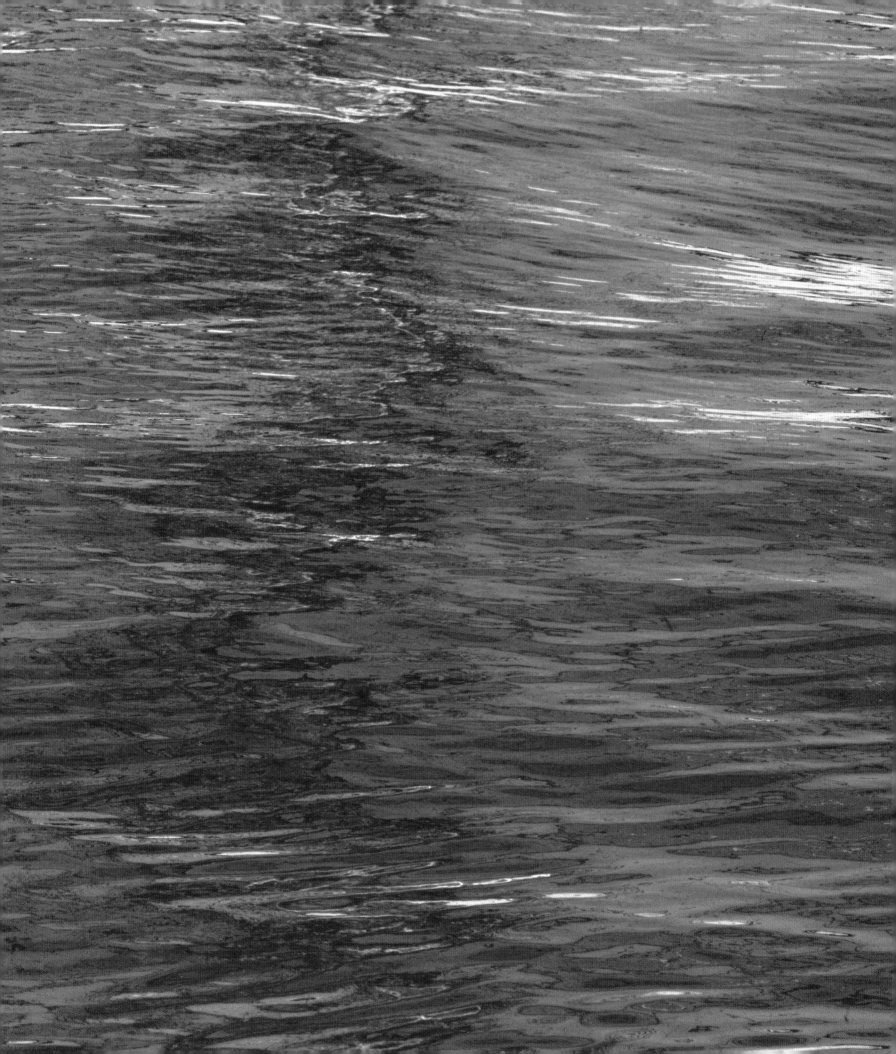

Gorch Fock being towed from the quay.

Lord Nelson, Gorch Fock, Kruzenshtern, Juan Sebastian de Elcano and *Europa* congregating for the start of the Cadiz to Bermuda race.

Europa leading *Kruzenshtern* at the start.

Gorch Fock heading to the New World.

Kruzenshtern dwarfing sailors aloft.

Eye of the Wind slipping by, while local spectators surround *Juan Sebastian de Elcano*.

Elcano, free and clear, sailing to Bermuda.

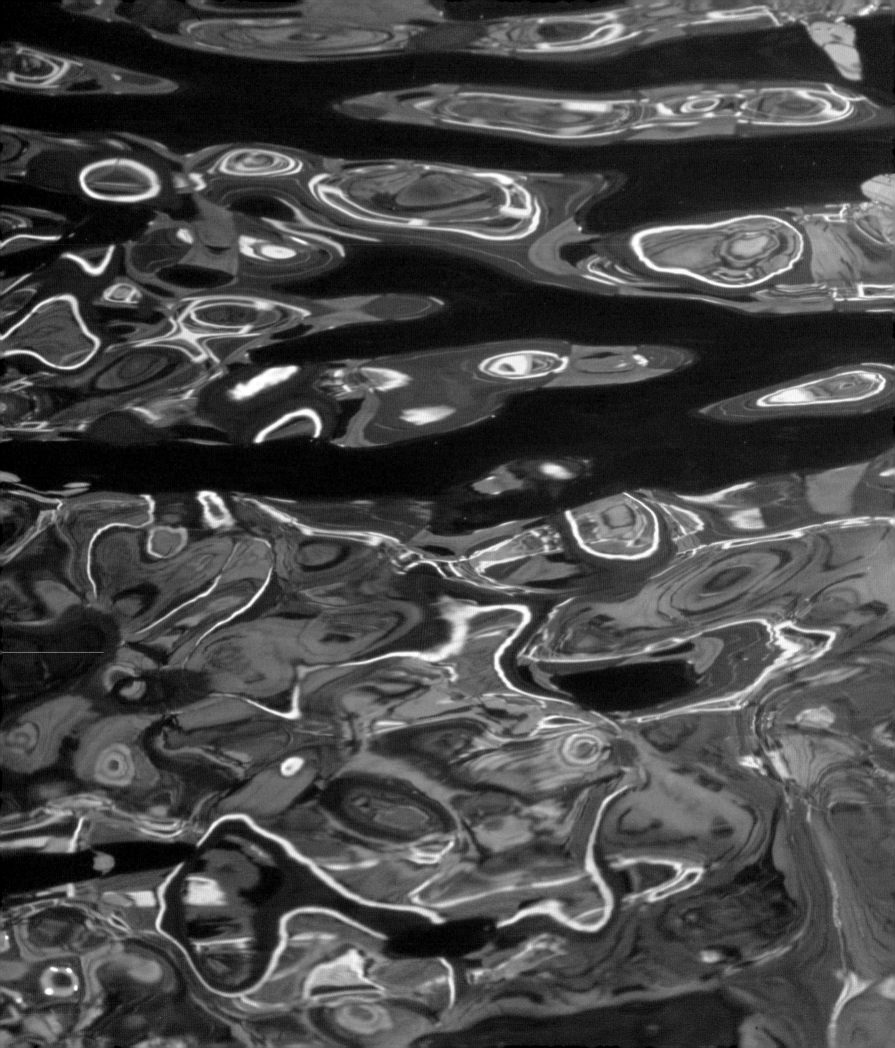

Bermuda

Gorch Fock, the first A-class ship to finish, at the
Royal Naval Dockyard, Bermuda.

Cadets on the aft deck of *Gorch Fock*.

Graphic detail of *Gorch Fock's* figurehead.

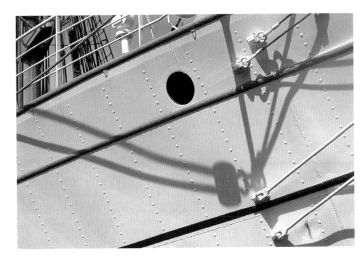

Detail of *Gorch Fock*.

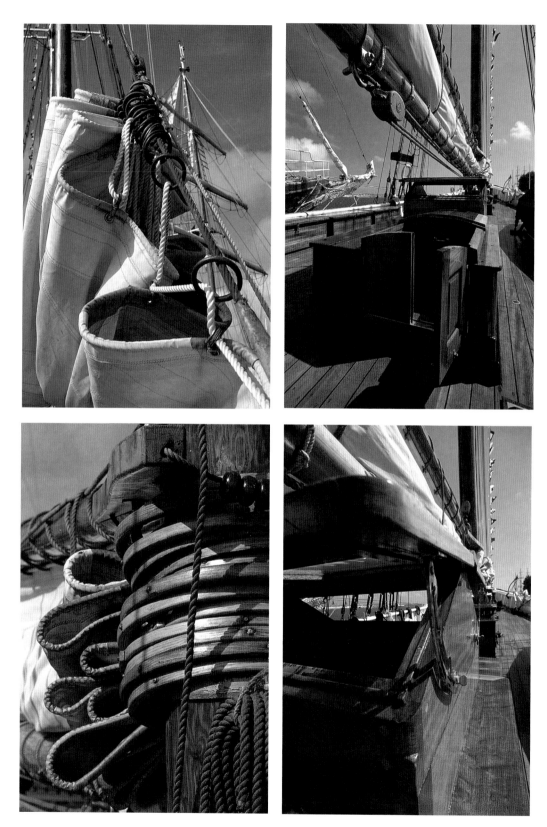

Bluenose II details.

Figurehead of *Asgard II*.

Exquisite detailing on *Amerigo Vespucci.*

Gilded stern of *Amerigo Vespucci.*

Crew muster on deck of *Amerigo Vespucci*.

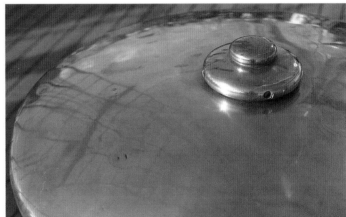

Yards and rigging.

Reflection in the capstan.

Lines made fast on the Fife rail.

"J" Class yacht *Endeavour* leaving St. George's Harbour, while C-class yachts shelter at the East End Mini Yacht Club.

Tug crew waiting in the harbour with *Dar Mlodziezy* resting at anchor.

Throwing a heaving line from *Libertad* to *Juan Sebastian de Elcano*.

Hauling a hawser.

The City of Hamilton evoking the past.

Provisioning *Lord Nelson.*

Eying activity in Hamilton Harbour.

Spectating, island style.

Painting the hull of *Kruzenshtern*.

Everything shipshape on *Jolie Brise*.

Almost.

Libertad crew relaxing aloft, while C-class vessels shelter at the Royal Bermuda Yacht Club.

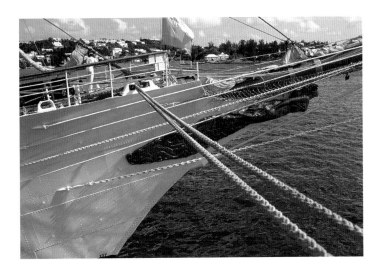

Watch officer viewing Hamilton Harbour from the foredeck of *Libertad.*

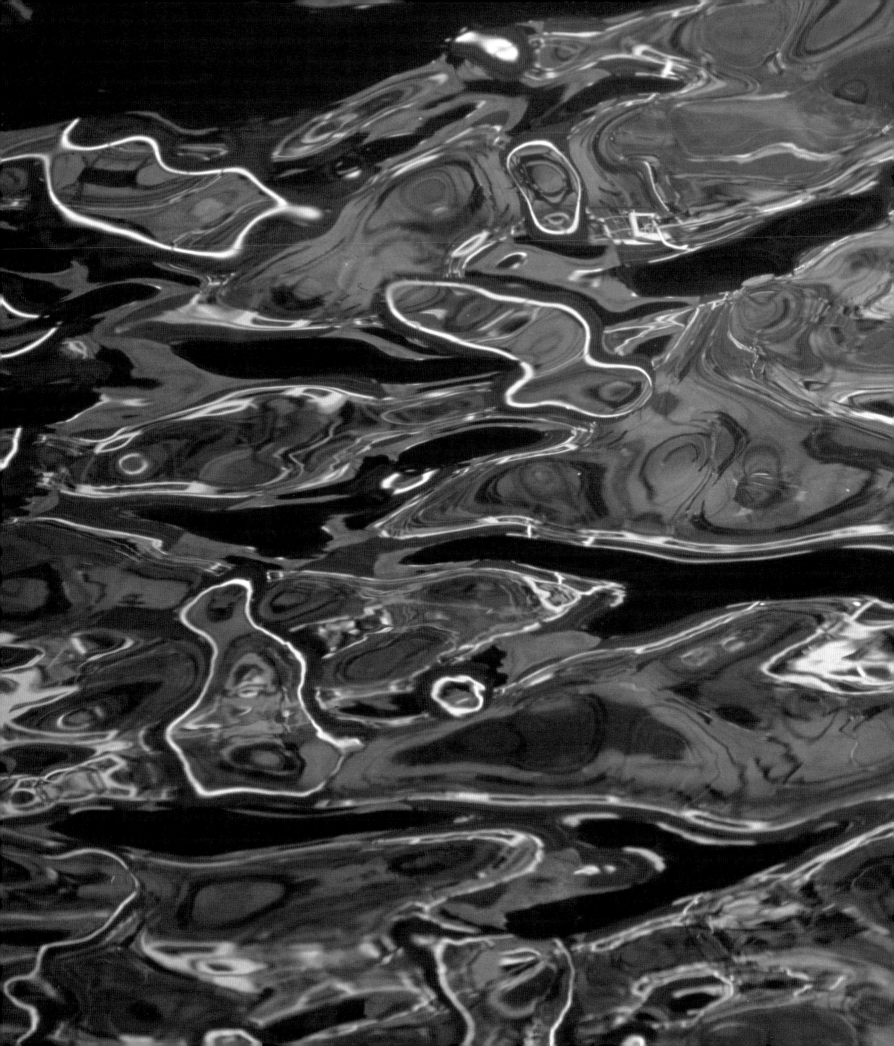

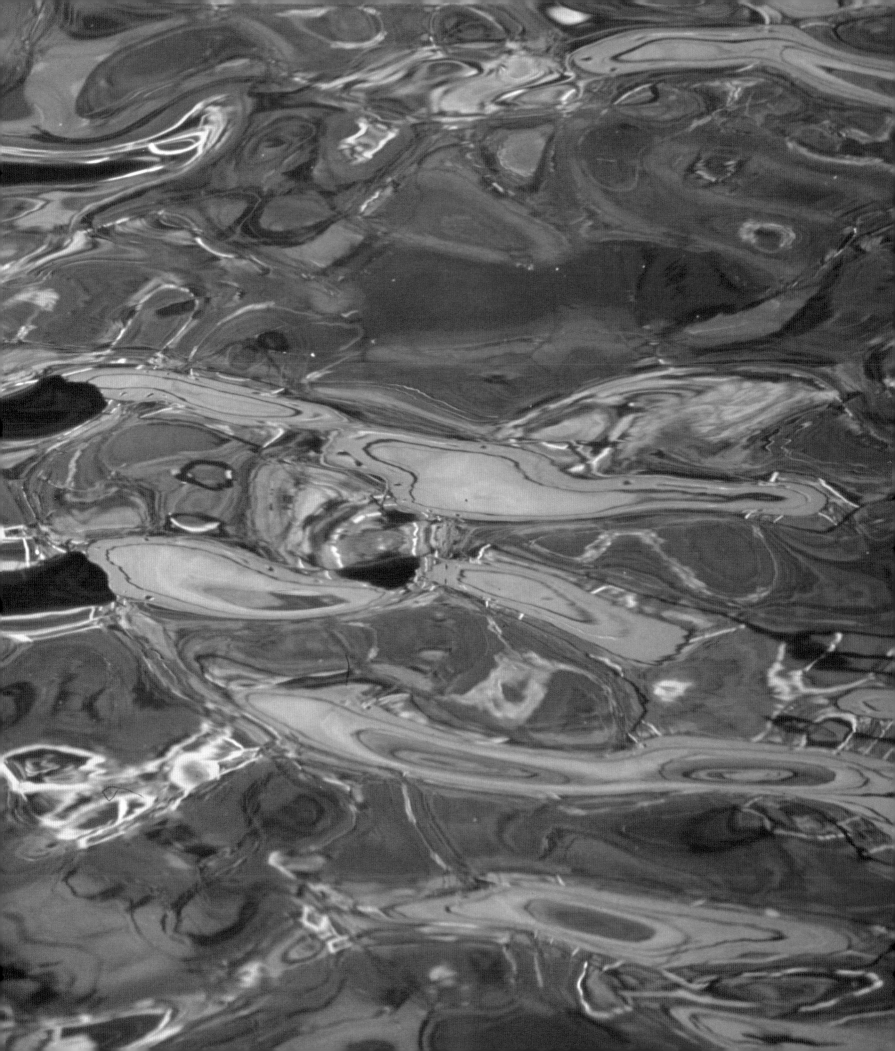

Dar Mlodziezy and *Kruzenshtern* passing Commissioner's House, Dockyard.

Jens Krogh, John Laing and *Jolie Brise* cruising along North Shore during the Parade of Sail.

Juan Sebastian de Elcano steering clear of Bermuda's infamous reefs.

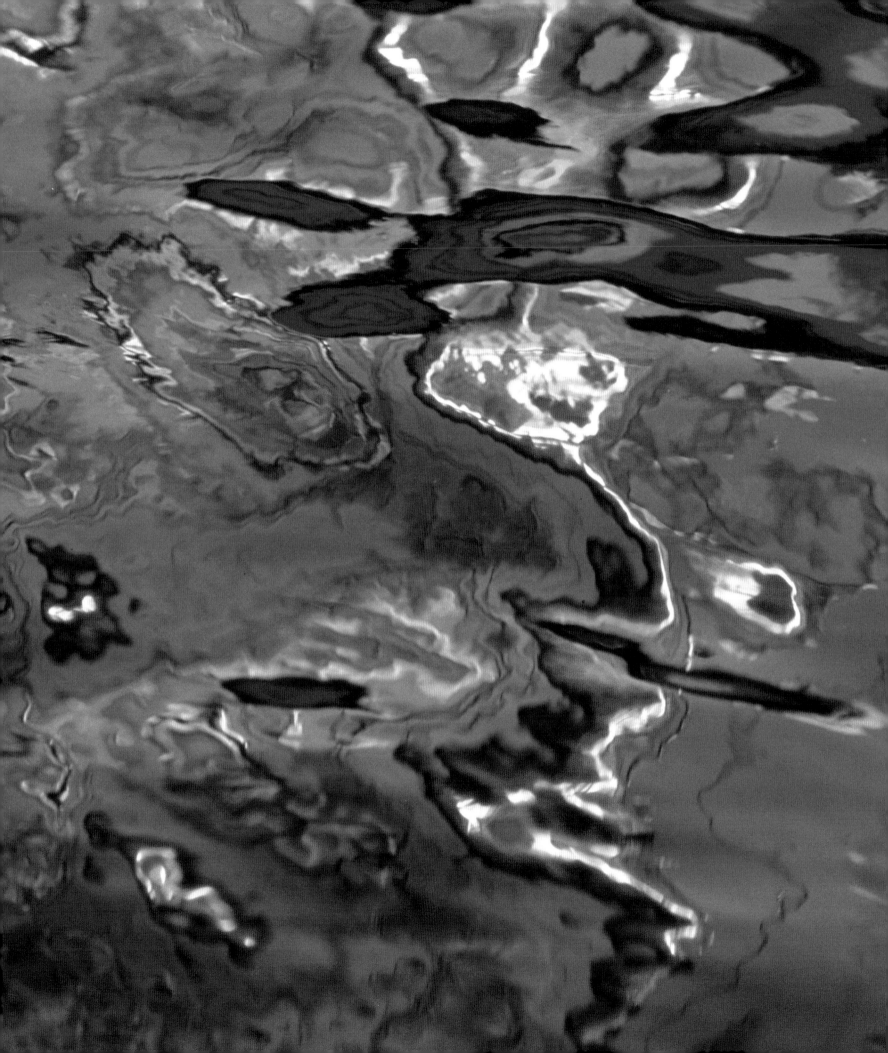

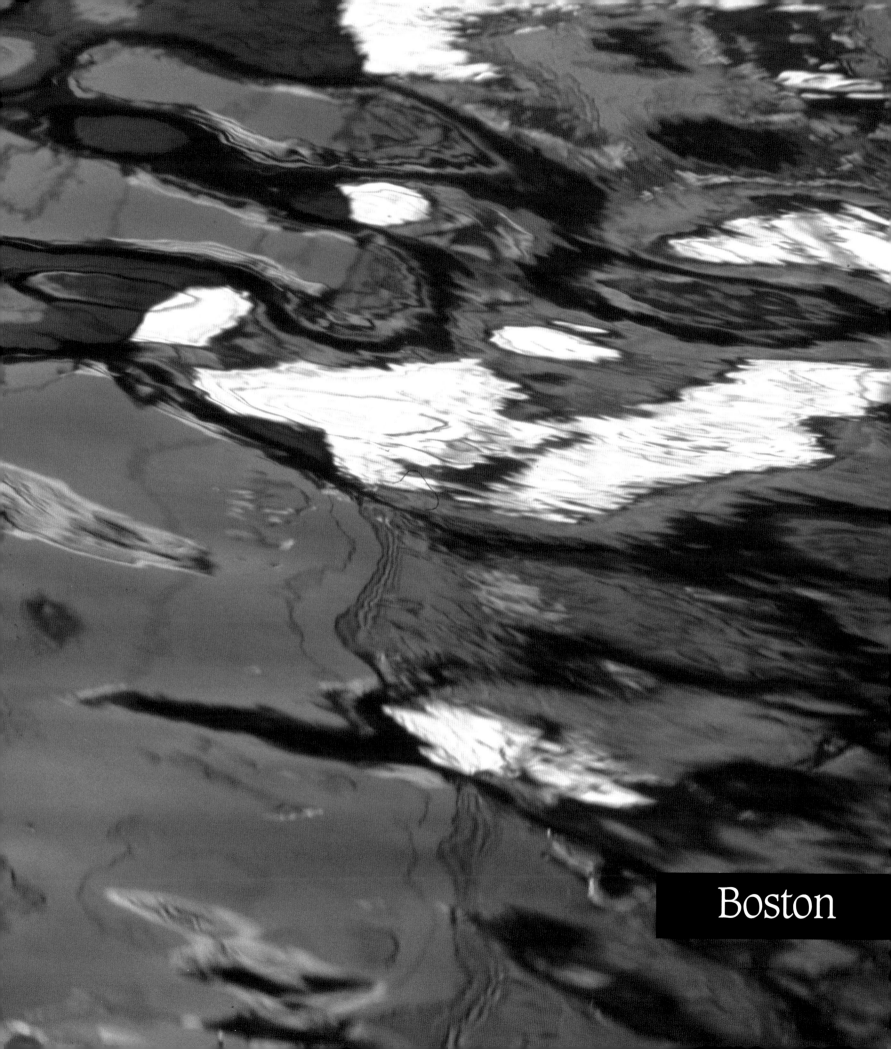

Boston

Flags flying at the Charleston Naval Yard.

Prospective mariner touring *USS Constitution.*

Mast and rigging through the American flag.

Rigging detail on *Kalmar Nyckel.*

Eclectic details of *Kalmar Nyckel*.

Bows bedecking Boston Harbour.

Wheel and skylight of *Bowdoin*.

Highlander Sea deckhouse and helm.

Deck of *Highlander Sea*.

Intricate carving on *Dewaruci*.

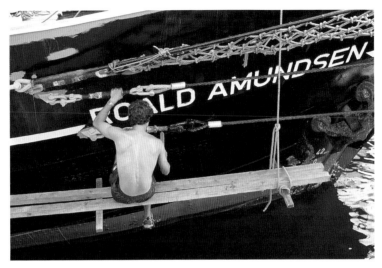

Wirebrushing and painting *Roald Amundsen.*

Fireworks silhouetting *Kalmar Nyckel* and *Fair Jeanne.*

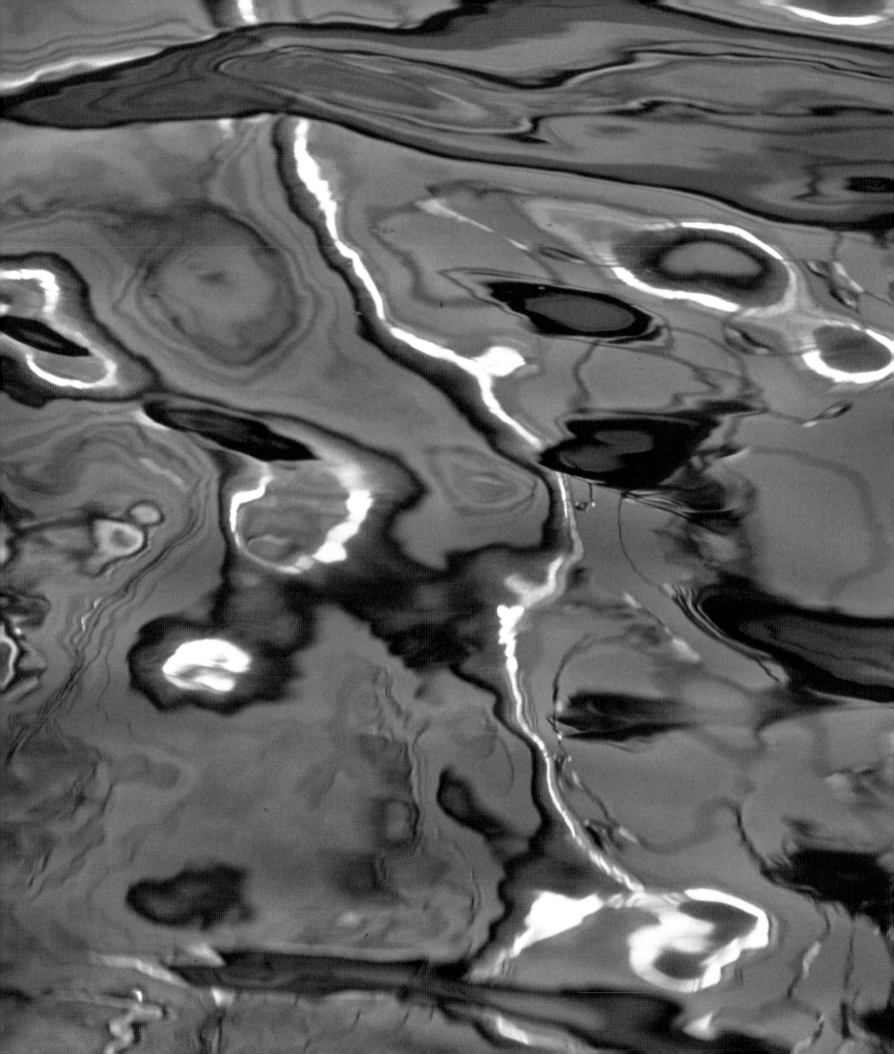

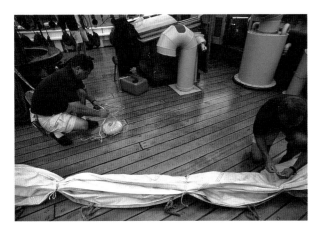

Aboard *Bluenose II.*

Stowing the fenders.

Cutting twine for gaskets.

Tying a gasket.

Raising the foresail.

Passing the fog shrouded *USS Constitution..*

Rocking and rolling through the fog.

Trying to sight a passing fishing trawler.

Bringing up and putting down.

Fog clearing on the way into Halifax Harbour.

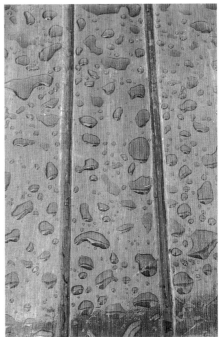

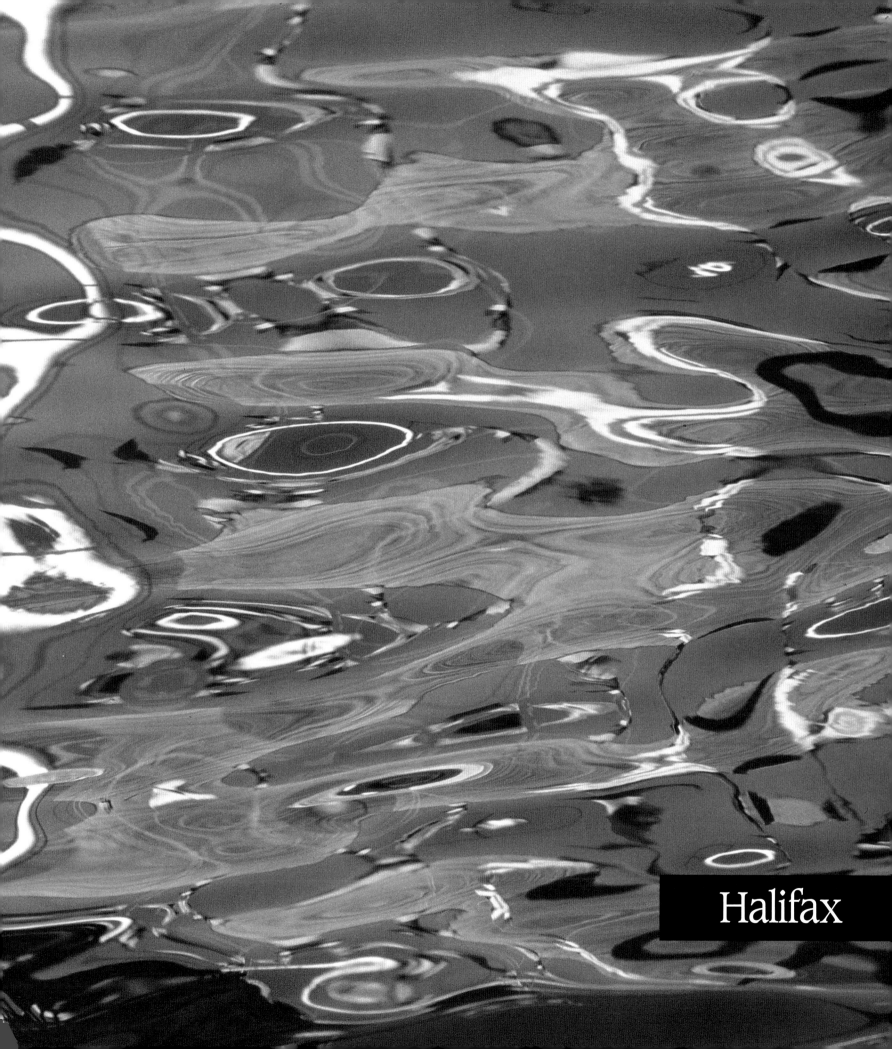

Halifax

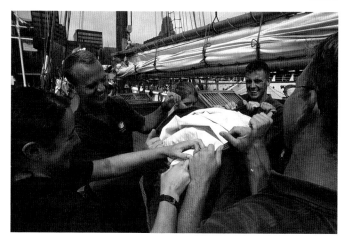

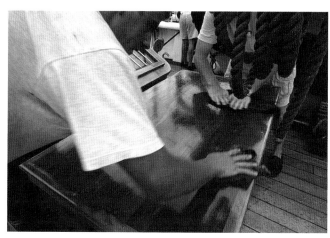

Downhauling the foresail.

Gasketing the foresail.

Captain Orval Banfield docking Bluenose II.

Casting a hawser to Lex MacKay.

Stowing sail.

Wiping the brightwork after washing.

Washing the deck.

Polishing the brass.

Catching up with maintainance before the
adoring crowd descends.

Sara Spike polishing a porthole.

Mike Silver reversing *Bluenose II* from it's berth to welcome ships into Halifax Harbour.

Keeping the deck clear.

Majestically gliding back into harbour.

Lofty viewing.

Juxtaposing ends of the Twentieth Century.

Stunning brass capstan on the Aft Deck of *Esmerelda*.

Figurehead of *Esmerelda*.

Wheel detail on *Sherman Zwicker.*

Aft helm of *Esmerelda.*

Turk's Head chafe plate.

Fo'c'sle entrance on *Sherman Zwicker*.

Halifax Harbour at dusk.

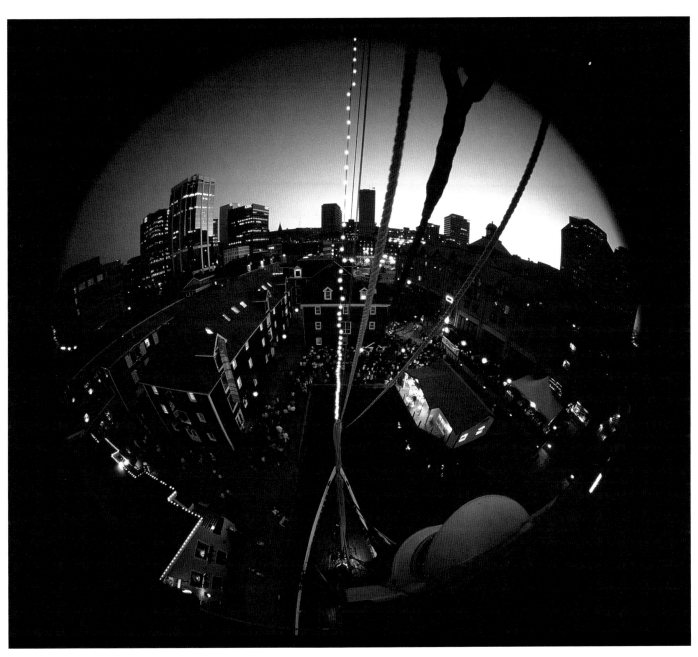

Skyline of Halifax and Privateer's Wharf from the rigging of *Highlander Sea*.

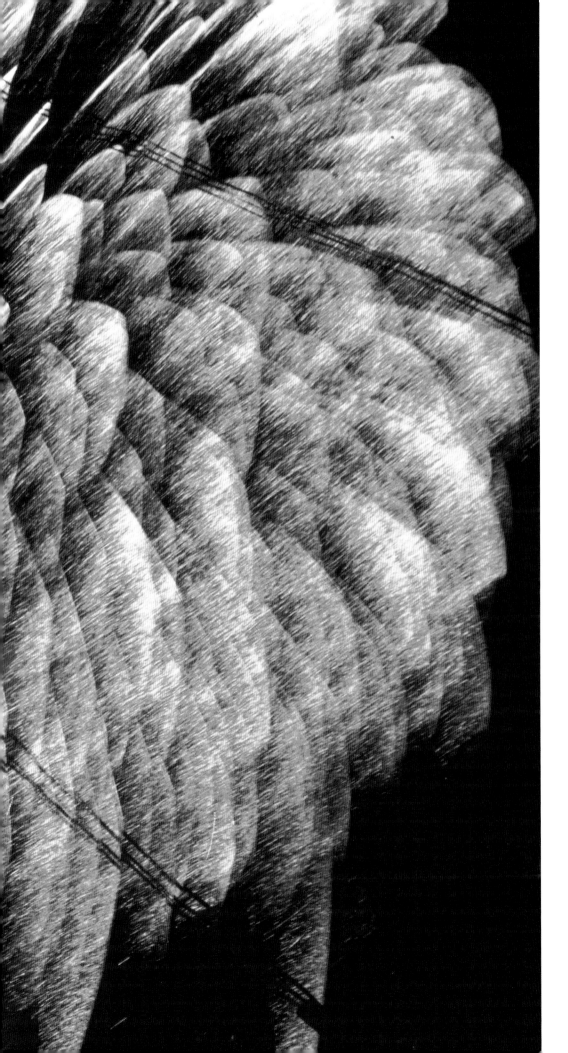

to the real world

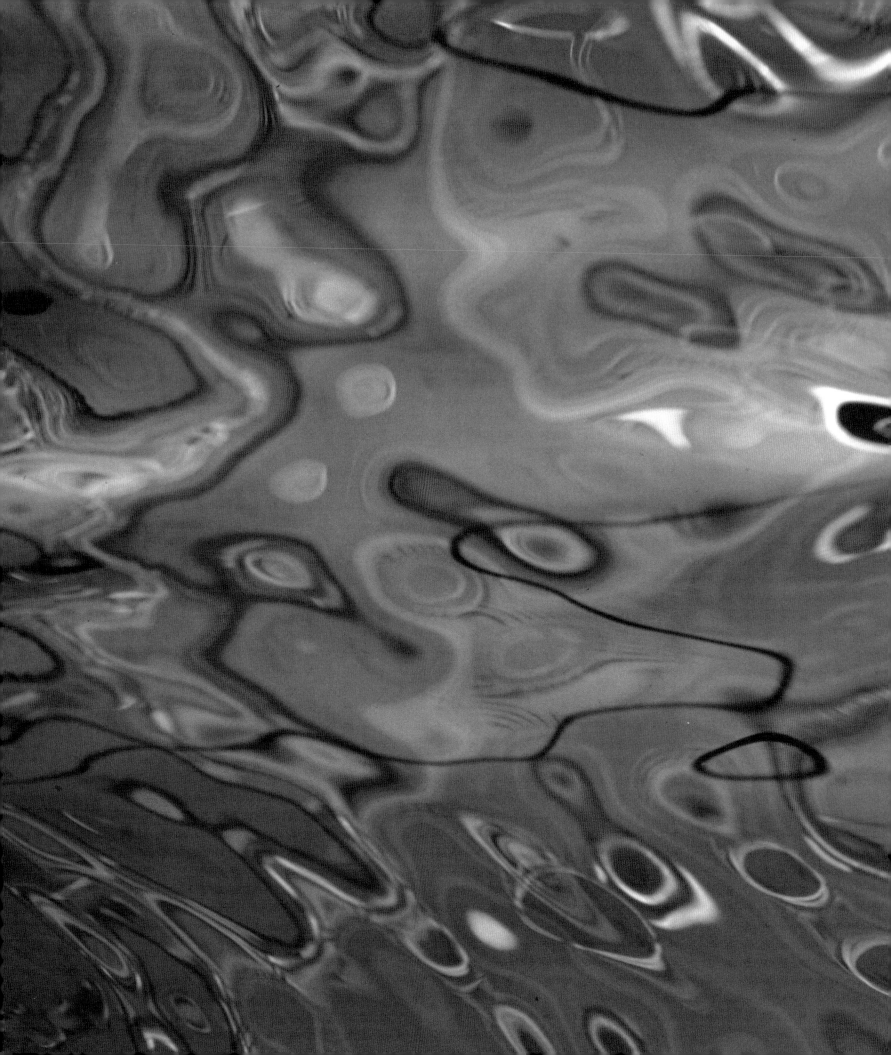

Parading in front of an orderly spectator fleet.

Gloria passing a packed waterfront.

Dar Mlodziezy, Europa, Lord Nelson, Bluenose II, Gloria, Mir and *Kruzenshtern* lining up for the start of the Halifax to Amsterdam race.

Squeezing across the startline.

Kruzenshtern and *Dar Mlodziezy* pulling away.

Pogoria, Gloria and *Mir* heading for the Old World.

*Jolie Bris*e sailing passed *Soren Larsen.*

Espying *Lord Nelson* through the mainsail of *Eye of the Wind.*

Jen Massie looking out.

Todd Jarrell standing on the Fore Topgallant Yard with *Akogare* ahead.

Checking the sail trim at sunset.

Going to bed alongside *Europa*.

But waking up with *Akogare*.

Enjoying a swim in a becalmed Atlantic Ocean on the second day out from Halifax.

Brad Jarrell working on the Flying Jib.

Tony Browne strumming away after the 4 to 8 watch.

Preparing dinner. Another tuna, a wahoo and a mahi-mahi also suffered the same fate during the crossing.

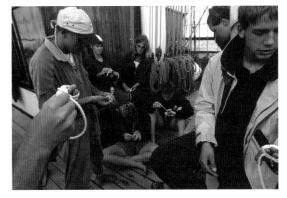

Rope tying classes with Jim Frost: Turk's Head (top and left)
and splicing (bottom).

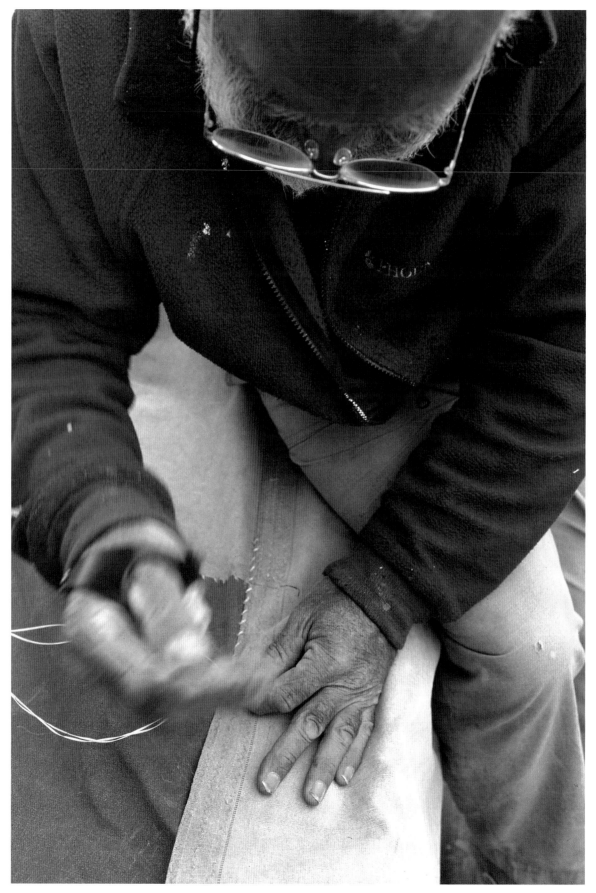

Tiger repairing the Flying Jib, which ripped at the start.

Savouring a beautiful harbinger.

Ominous clouds approaching.

Bolting storm shutters to the Galley Deckhouse.

Tiger holding course in gale conditions.

Wave breaking over the bow.

The forty hour gale proved a little traumatic for a few of the trainees - some had never seen the ocean. There was no respite but the *Eye* ploughed through with grace. Watches continued as usual and meals were delivered on time - eating them was another matter entirely.

Pitching and rolling.

Spectacular sight at the end of the wind tunnel.

Unfastening the Flying Jib for repairs - again.

Preparing to lower the Fore Course for repairs.

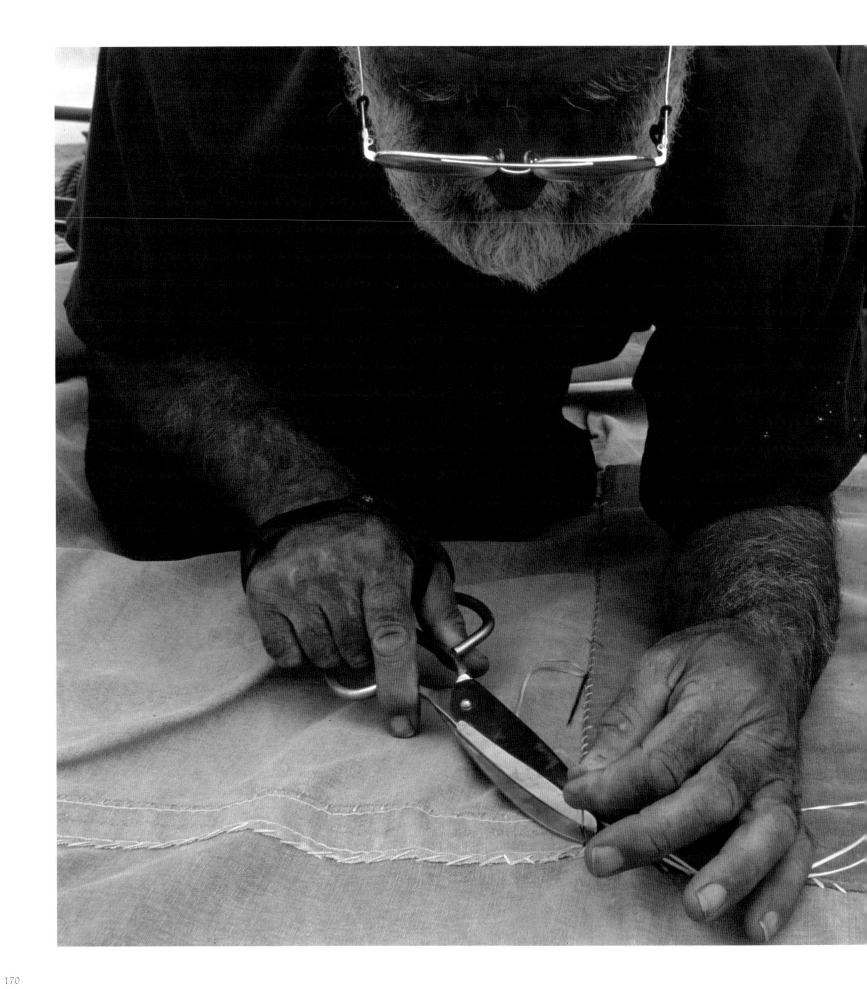

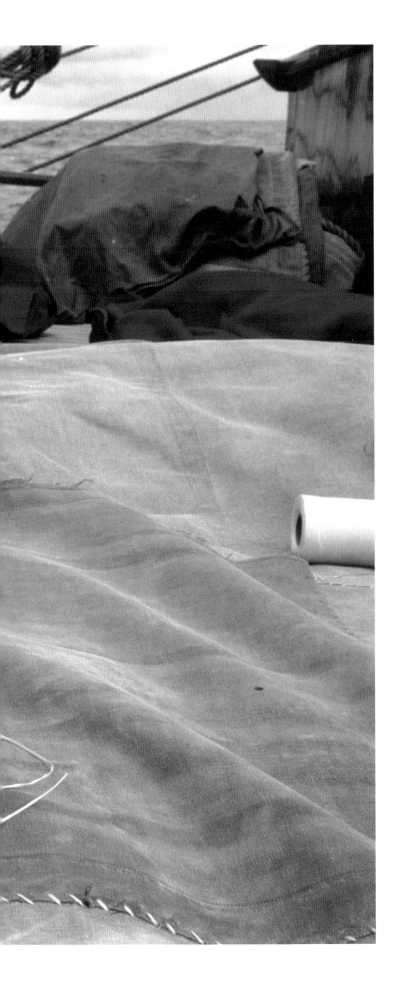

Tiger repairing the Fore Course.

Reshackling the Fore Course.

And hauling it back aloft.

Tanya Johnston washing the rails.

Jen Massie rinsing the Aft Deckhouse.

Looking down from the Fore Tops.

Morning dew clinging to the 'Dive Shack' door.

Pastel shades at day's end.

Dolphins gracefully avoiding the Dolphin Striker.

Learning to tie a Wall Knot.

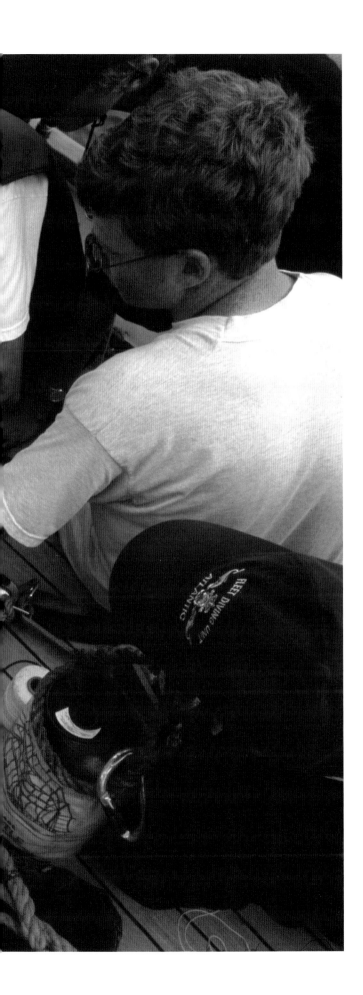

Chef, Gill Allen, being serenaded by the 'Splice Girls' on her birthday.

Sennet braids.

Turk's Head knot on the Mainsail Boom.

Tiger enjoying a rare moment of peace and quiet at home.

A rare phenomenon - 'Greenflash' at sea.

Tony Browne unjamming a line caught in the Stunsail Halyard Block.

Then coming down to deck.

Jenny Kearsley splicing while Tony stays on course.

Sweating the Stunsail halyard.

Bosun Ellis Robertson tarring lines aloft.

Approaching the finish line under full sail.

Whipping a bitter end.

Figurehead of the *Eye of the Wind* through the Widowmaker.

Making a temporary impression.

Brad Jarrell performing a line check at the end of watch.

Making the most of every bit of breeze.

Passing another ship in the English Channel.

Sighting the Cliffs of Dover from the Main Tops.

The imposing chalk cliffs.

Goodwin Sands lightship warning mariners of the treacherous graveyard beyond.

Reflection in the *Eye's* wheel. Polishing the brass starts a couple of days before arrival in port.

Compass binnacle starting to look good again.

Kathryn Alton hauling away.

Marlena Turner and Chris Veenstra gasketing the Fore Topgallant.

Part of the fleet resting in Scheveningen after the long passage across the North Atlantic.

Dar Mlodziezy in Scheveningen.

Sailing in a fresh North Sea breeze before making way to Amsterdam.

210

Jolie Brise heading for the entrance to the Grand Canal.

Feeling decidedly skeletal in the convoy on the final approach.

Sighting *Sedov*, the largest tallship in the world.

Throwing welcome refreshment to the crew of *Europa*.

Europa preparing to pull alongside *Sedov*.

Waiting in the lock before entering the Grand Canal.

Entering the Grand Canal.

Furling the sails for the last time.

Libertad berthing amid the melee.

Crew of *Libertad* Manning the Yards.

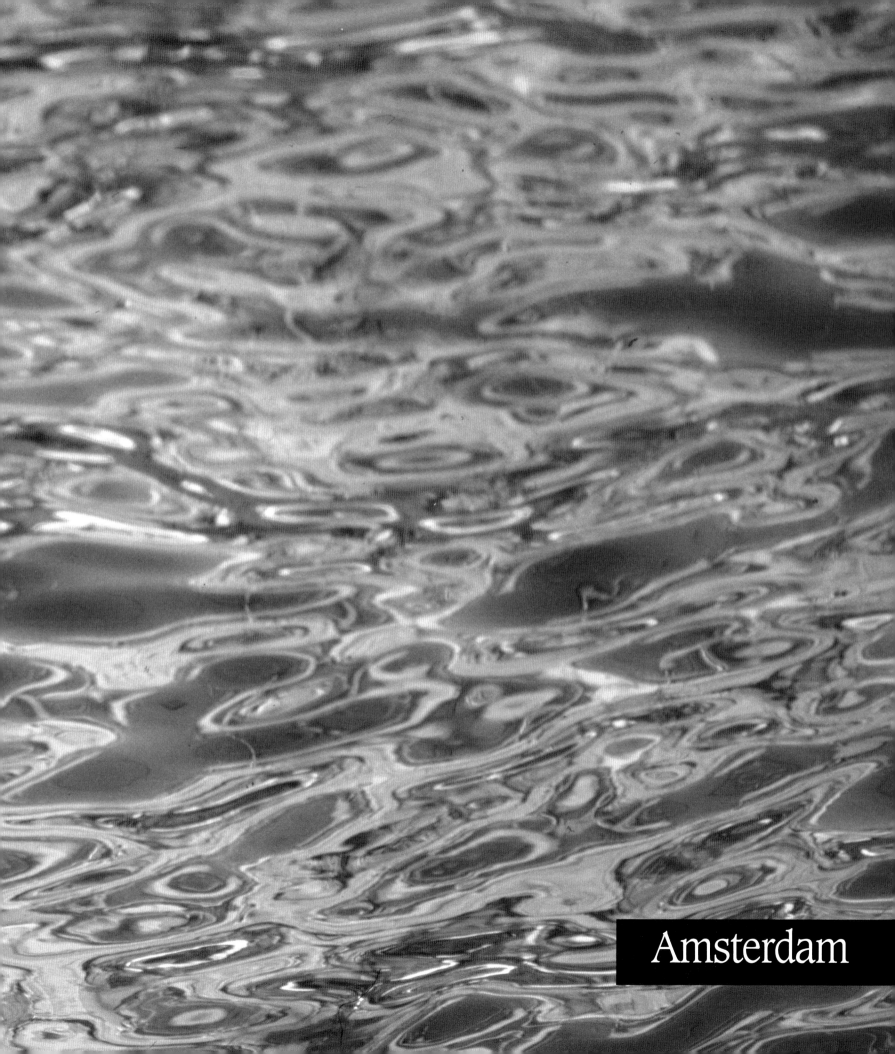

Amsterdam

Toby Marris, skipper of *Jolie Brise*, relaxing after winning the four and a half month odyssey.

Christian Radich from the stern of *Jolie Brise*.

Spectating from dawn...

...to dusk, Dutch style.

The merry going round and round.

Revelling in nostalgia.

And finally...tranquility.

Enjoying hospitality aboard *Libertad* while *Sedov* rests easily.

Akogare calmly resting before the long journey home.

The final reminiscence.

Tall Ships 2000 Race

Race Leg	Date	Ports
Race 1	April 16	Southampton, England - Cadiz, Spain
Race 2	April 23	Genoa, Italy - Cadiz, Spain
Race 3	May 7	Cadiz, Spain - Bermuda
Cruise in Company	June 12	Bermuda - Boston, USA
Race 4	July 16	Boston,USA - Halifax, Canada
Race 5	July 24	Halifax, Canada - Amsterdam, Netherlands

Vessel	Nation	Class	1	2	3	CinC	4	5
Akogare	Japan	B	●	●	●	●	○	○
Alaska	Malta	CII	●	○	●	●	●	●
Amerigo Vespucci	Italy	A	●	○	○	○	○	●
Arethusa	UK	CII	○	●	○	○	○	○
Arung Samudera	Indonesia	B	●	○	○	○	○	○
Asgard II	Ireland	AII	○	●	○	○	○	○
Blitz	Italy	CIII	●	○	○	○	○	○
Bluenose II	Canada	B	●	●	●	○	○	●
Brilliant	USA	CI	●	●	●	●	○	○
Californian	USA	B	●	●	●	●	○	●
Capitan Miranda	Uruguay	A	●	●	●	●	○	○
Chessie	USA	CII	●	●	●	●	○	●
Concordia	Bahamas	A	●	●	●	○	○	○
Concordia	Norway	C1	●	●	●	●	○	○
Dar Mlodziezy	Poland	A	○	●	○	○	○	○
Dasher	UK	CIII	○	●	○	○	○	○
Eendracht	Netherlands	A	●	●	●	●	○	○
Eleanor Mary	UK	CI	○	●	○	○	○	○
Esprit	Germany	CII	○	●	○	○	○	○
Europa	Netherlands	A	○	●	○	○	○	○
Eye of the Wind	UK	AII	○	●	○	○	○	○

Vessel	Nation	Class	1	2	3	CinC	4	5
Fair Jeanne	Canada	AII	●	●	●	●	○	●
Freelord	Czech Republic	CIII	●	○	○	○	●	●
Gloria	Columbia	A	●	●	●	●	●	○
Gorch Fock	Germany	A	●	●	○	○	●	●
Gulliver of Southampton	UK	CIII	○	●	●	○	○	○
Harvey Gamage	USA	CI	●	●	●	○	○	●
Hebe III	Czech Republic	CIII	●	○	○	○	○	○
Highlander Sea	Canada	B	●	●	●	○	○	●
Ice Maiden	UK	CII	○	●	○	○	○	○
Idea Due	Italy	CIII	●	○	●	○	○	●
Jens Krogh	Denmark	CI	○	●	○	○	○	○
John Laing	UK	CIII	○	●	○	○	○	○
Jolie Brise	UK	CI	○	●	○	○	○	○
Juan Sebastian de Elcano	Spain	A	●	●	○	○	●	●
Kaiwo Maru	Japan	A	●	●	●	●	○	●
Kaliakra	Bulgaria	A	●	○	●	●	●	●
Kruzenshtern	Russia	A	○	●	○	○	○	○
Kukri	UK	CIII	○	●	○	○	○	○
Lettie G Howard	USA	CI	●	●	●	●	○	●
Libertad	Argentina	A	●	●	●	○	○	●
Lord Nelson	UK	A	○	●	○	○	○	●
Maiden	UK	CII	○	●	○	○	○	○
Mendrugo	Jersey	CI	●	●	○	●	●	●
Mir	Russia	A	○	●	○	○	○	○
Mist of Avalon	Canada	CI	●	●	●	○	○	●
Misty Isles	USA	CI	●	●	●	●	○	●
Moonspray	UK	CIII	○	●	●	●	●	●
Morning Star of Revelation	UK	CI	○	●	○	○	○	●
Niagara	USA	A	●	●	●	●	○	●
NV Hamburg	Germany	CIII	●	●	●	●	○	○
Ocean Spirit of Moray	UK	CII	○	●	○	●	○	○
Oosterschelde	Netherlands	B	●	●	●	●	○	●
Pandora	Italy	CI	●	○	●	○	○	●
Peter von Danzig	Germany	CIII	○	●	○	○	●	●
Picton Castle	Greek Islands	A	●	●	●	○	○	●
Pogoria	Poland	A	●	○	●	○	○	○
Pride of Baltimore II	USA	B	●	●	●	●	○	○
Roald Amundsen	Germany	A	●	●	○	○	○	○
Rona II	UK	CIII	○	●	○	○	○	○
Rose 'HMS'	USA	A	●	●	●	●	○	●
Sagittario	Italy	CII	●	○	●	●	●	●
Sarie Marais of Plym	UK	CIII	○	●	○	○	○	○
Soren Larsen	NZ	AII	●	●	●	●	○	●
Spirit of Massachusetts	USA	B	●	●	●	●	○	●
Stella Polare	Italy	CIII	●	○	○	○	○	○
St Lawrence II	Canada	AII	●	●	●	●	○	●
Walross III Berlin	Germany	CIII	●	●	●	●	○	●
Westward	USA	B	●	●	●	○	●	●
Zenobe Gramme	Belgium	CII	○	●	○	○	○	○
Zjawa IV	Poland	CII	●	●	●	○	○	●

Published by:

Just Clicked Publications,
Bermuda House Lane,
95 Front Street,
Hamilton HM 12,
Bermuda.

Tel: 1 441 292-3295

www.imacsmith.com

ISBN 0-9688838-0-X

First Edition

Also available by the author:

2000 Limited Edition books: embossed leather, gilded
and casebound.
200 Limited Edition Archival prints for each image.

Other books by the author:

Held in Trust, 1989
A Scape to Bermuda, 1991
Bermuda Triangles, 1993
Bermuda Gardens & Houses, 1996

Printed in the England by
Butler & Tanner Limited,
The Selwood Printing Works,
Caxton Road,
Frome,
Somerset,

For information on the Tall Ships 2000 Race visit:

www.tallships2000.com
www.ista.com
www.eyeofthewind.com
www.joliebrise.com
www.bluenose2.ns.ca
www.imacsmith.com

Camera equipment:

Olympus OM 4T
Zuiko 8mm Fisheye f2.8
Zuiko 18mm f3.5
Zuiko 21mm f2
Zuiko 24mm Shift f3.5
Zuiko 35mm shift f2.8
Zuiko 35-80 f2.8
Zuiko 85-250mm
Zuiko 500mm f8

Olympus C-2500L

Hasselblad X-Pan
Fuji 45mm f4

Nikonos V w/35mm f2.5

Mamiya 645 AF
Mamiya 45mm AF
Mamiya 85mm AF
Mamiya 120mm AF
Mamiya 300mm AF

PhaseOne LightPhase

Film: Fuji Provia 100F

Bluenose II:

Standing from left: Scott Webber (Second Officer), Phil Watson (Chief Officer), Lauranne MacNeill, Captain Orval Banfield (Chief Engineer), Reg Barkhouse (Chief Cook), Bill Foster, Kelly Gilchrist, Spencer Dewar, Zoe Nudell, Glenn Fougere, Andrew Giomo, Mike Gough, Sara Spike, Andre St. Pierre.
Seated: Jason Keddy (Bosun), Jason McNaught.

Eye of the Wind:

Top row from left: Lucas Brotz, Steve Barnes, Andrew Eaton, Chris Veenstra, Louis Brenn, Nikki Olson Suttie Grant, Tanya Jonston, Pixie Cram.
Middle row from left: Reyn Amos, Brad Jarrell (Crew), Robert Hamon, Todd Jarrell (Crew), Jen Massie, Marlena Turner, Natalie Haras, Ed Callendar, Marcus Piotrowski, Kathryn Alton, Brett Cowden, Jonathan Levy, Captain Anthony 'Tiger' Timbs.
Bottom row from left: Gill Allen (Chef), Bobby Tulloch (Engineer), Ellis Robertson (Bosun), Tamara Milberg, Jenny Kearsley (Crew), Jim Frost (Second Mate), Gwyneth Therwell, Laura Craik (Crew), Tony Browne (First Mate).

Sincere thanks to:

The millions - people, organizations, companies, governments - who organized, supported, helped and spectated to make the Tall Ships 2000 Race a truly peaceful global event.

The *Bluenose II* Trust and Senator Wilfred Moore for allowing me aboard this Canadian icon. A special thanks to the captain and crew for making the journey so enjoyable, for their accomodation in Halifax and their unfailing humour. Also, my thanks to Lex MacKay, who keeps everything on an even keel.

The *Eye of the Wind*: Captain 'Tiger' Timbs, a living legend, without whom this book would not be. For sacrificing his privacy in allowing me aboard to record this incredible journey.

The crew of the *Eye*: Tony, Jim, Laura, Ellis, Jenny, Bobby, Gill, Brad and Todd for putting me to work and teaching me. Your patience, tolerance and expertise made a huge difference in many peoples' lives during the Tall Ships 2000 Race.

Brian Billings and John Wadson at Tall Ships 2000-Bermuda for their cheerful enthusiasm, help and support. And also for positively changingthe lives of so many young Bermudians.

Bruce Mitchell at Fuji Photo Film USA for generously providing film. Jennifer Davalos at Fuji for kindly providing the FineScan 2750 scanner responsible for achieving the final quality of the images.

Carsten Steenberg at Phase One for hoisting the sails.

All the photographers who have selflessly helped me to see more clearly: Particularly, Mark Emmerson, Sam Abell and especially Douglas Dubler, who is a great mentor and friend. I am humbled and eternally grateful.

Nigel Pert for the Southampton images and Alexis Komenda for the Genoa images. This book would not be complete without their knowledge of sailing and their subsequent vision.

Hugh Murray-Mason at Insight Visual Communications for his sage advice in the design of this book and for his friendship and sense of humour.

Joy Pratt and David Cox for providing welcome and convenient shelter in Charleston and London respectively.

My family, who keep me grounded. Especially; Roger and Marietta Snell for the luxury of a bed and shower after six weeks of bunking; Jeremy Snell of Butler & Tanner for his help and advice in the creation of this volume; Iain Macdonald-Smith for graciously agreeing to write the foreword; and, as always, my parents.

All my friends for their love, support, encouragement and inspiration over the years, without whom I could not have contemplated this journey. I am truly blessed.